ISBN 978-0-259-30636-8
PIBN 10813180

1 MONTH OF
FREE
READING

at

www.ForgottenBooks.com

By purchasing this book you are eligible for one month membership to ForgottenBooks.com, giving you unlimited access to our entire collection of over 1,000,000 titles via our web site and mobile apps.

To claim your free month visit: www.forgottenbooks.com/free813180

THE

Teaching of English Law

AT

Universities.

BY

JAMES BRADLEY THAYER, LL.D.

WELD PROFESSOR OF LAW AT HARVARD UNIVERSITY.

Read at Detroit August 27, 1895, as the Chairman's Address, before the Section on Legal Education of the American Bar Association.

BOSTON:

LITTLE, BROWN, AND COMPANY.

1895.

9

The Author

TEACHING OF ENGLISH LAW

UNIVERSITIES.

IN so great a country as ours, so wide and so diversified, it is peculiarly well, now and then, to gather together from far and near,
and meet on a common footing as Americans. And so we have come
now to this beautiful city, a novel and strange place to many of us, to
breathe for a day or two this exhilarating atmosphere of a common
nationality, the broad and general air that blows not merely here
or there in our country, but everywhere; to think the thoughts
and interchange the sentiments that concern us as American
lawyers. For myself, I have been chiefly moved, in coming here
from the far-away sea-coast of Maine, by the desire to say a few
words towards urging a very thorough and learned study of our
English law, and the maintenance of schools of law which conform
in all respects to the highest University standards of work.

We, in America, have carried legal education much farther
than it has gone in England. There the systematic teaching of

---

¹ An address, read at Detroit, August 27, 1895, as Chairman of the Section on
Legal Education of the American Bar Association.

The reader is requested to observe that this paper does not deal with mere method
of teaching, or with any differences which may be supposed to be appropriate in under
graduate instruction as contrasted with that of postgraduate and professional courses
It is directed to the University teaching of English law, by whatever methods carried
on, in whatever departments, and for whatever purpose. The author had chiefly ir
mind the "law schools" properly so called ; that is to say, schools aiming directly a
professional education.

law in schools is but faintly developed. Here it is elaborate, widely favored, rapidly extending. Why is this? Not because we originated this method. We transplanted an English root. and nurtured and developed it, while at home it was suffered to languish and die down. It was the great experiment in the University teaching of our law at Oxford, in the third quarter of the eighteenth century, and the publication, a little before the American Revolution, of the results of that experiment, which furnished the stimulus and the exemplar for our own early attempts at systematic legal education. The opportunities and the material here for any thorough work of this sort in the offices of lawyers were slight. " I never dreamed," said Chancellor Kent, in speaking of the state of things in New York, even so late as the period when he was appointed to the bench of the Supreme Court of that State in 1798, " of volumes of reports and written opinions. Such things were not then thought of. . . . There were no reports or State precedents. I first introduced a thorough examination of cases, and written opinions." [1] But wisdom, skill, experience, and an acquaintance with English books were not wanting in the legal profession here ; and Blackstone's great achievement awakened the utmost interest and enthusiasm on both sides of the water, — his success in the really Herculean task of redeeming to orderly statement and to an approximately scientific form, the disordered bulk of our common law. " I retired to a country village," Chancellor Kent tells us, in speaking of the breaking up of Yale College by the war, where he was a student in 1779, " and, finding Blackstone's Commentaries, I read the four volumes. . . . The work inspired me at the age of fifteen with awe, and I fondly determined to be a lawyer." As a student in the office of the Attorney-General of New York, in 1781 and later, he says that he read Blackstone " again and again." [2] Blackstone's lectures were begun in 1753, when the author, then only thirty years old, a discouraged barrister of seven years' standing, had retired from Westminster and settled down to academic work at Oxford. On the death of Viner he was made, in 1758, the first professor of English law at any English University ; and he published his first volume of lectures in 1765. " There is abundant evidence," if we may rely upon the authority of Dr. Hammond, whose language I quote, " of the immediate absorption of nearly twenty-five hundred copies of the commentaries in the

[1] Green Bag, vii. 157.   [2] Ibid. 153.

thirteen colonies before the Declaration of Independence. . . . Upon all questions of private law, at least, this work stood for the law itself throughout the country, and . . . exercised an influence upon the jurisprudence of the new nation which no other work has since enjoyed." [1]   This great result, it should be observed, was the work of a young enthusiast in legal education, a scholar and a University man, who had the genius to see that English law was worthy to be taught on a footing with other sciences, and as other systems of law had been taught in the Universities of other countries.

Blackstone's example was immediately followed here, and was soon further developed in the form which he had urged upon the authorities at Oxford, but urged in vain, — that of a separate college or school of law.   In 1779, the year after Blackstone had published the eighth and final edition of his lectures, and only a year before his death, a chair of law was founded in Virginia, at William and Mary College, by the efforts of Jefferson, then a visitor of the institution ; and in the same year Isaac Royall of Massachusetts, then a resident in London, made his will, giving property to Harvard College for establishing there that professorship of law which still bears his name.   In 1790, Wilson gave law lectures at the University of Pennsylvania.   The Litchfield Law School, established about 1784, was not a University school; yet if it be true, as is not improbable, that it was the natural outgrowth of an office overcrowded with students, it may well be conjectured that Blackstone's undertaking chiefly shaped and sustained it.   At any rate his lectures appear to have been the chief references of the instructors at Litchfield.   Hammond, in referring to a collection of *verbatim* notes of lectures at the Litchfield school in 1817, representing, as he conceives, " the exact teaching " of the professors of that time, says " that the references to Blackstone not only outnumber those of any other book, but may be said to outnumber all the rest together." [2]

In England little progress was made for a century.   Blackstone's plan for a law College at Oxford was not carried out, and he resigned, disappointed, in 1766.   The conservatism of a powerful profession, absorbed in the mere business of its calling, itself untrained in the learned or scientific study of law, and unconscious of the need of such training, did not yield to or much consider the

---

[1] 1 Hammond's Blackstone, ix.   [2] Ibid. x., note.

suggestions of what had already been done at Oxford. The old method of office apprenticeship was not broken up. The profession was contented with Blackstone's Commentaries, as if these had done all that could be done and had made the full and final restatement of the law. The student simply added to his ordinary work the reading of these volumes.

But the more enlightened members of our profession in England have keenly felt the backward state of things there. One of the greatest of them, Sir Richard Bethell, afterwards Lord Chancellor Westbury, on taking his seat as president of the Juridical Society forty years ago, lamented the neglect of legal science in England and the strange indifference of the profession to the pursuit of it. Lawyers, he says,[1] " are members of a profession who, from the beginning to the end of their lives, ought to regard themselves as students of the most exalted branch of knowledge, Moral Philosophy embodied and applied in the laws and institutions of a great people. There is no other class or order in the community," he adds, " on whom so much of human happiness depends, or whose pursuits and studies are so intimately connected with the progress and well-being of mankind." In enumerating the causes of this failure to appreciate the dignity of their calling, he names as one of the chief of them, " the want of a systematic and well-arranged course of legal education. . . . It belongs," he adds, " to the Universities of England and to the Inns of Court to fill the void; but for centuries the duty has remained unperformed." It still remains very imperfectly performed. But England is moving in the direction that Blackstone pointed, and in its own way will yet solve the problem. Admirable work is going forward there now; and how full a sympathy the leaders in it entertain for our own efforts is shown by the coming of Sir Frederick Pollock this summer to take part in the exercises at Harvard, on occasion of the celebration of Dean Langdell's twenty-fifth anniversary. He crossed the ocean for that mere purpose, and returned as soon as it was accomplished.

On this side of the water, while the training of our profession continued for a long time to be the old one of office apprenticeship and reading, the new conception — new as regards English law— of systematic study at the Universities, has had continuous life, and has borne abundant fruit. If it has sometimes languished,

---

[1] 1 Jurid. Soc. Pap. 1.

and here and there been intermittent, it has always lived and thriven somewhere; and at last it has so commended itself that there is no longer much occasion to argue its merits. Few now come openly forward to deny or doubt them.

This, then, is our American distinction, to have accepted and carried for a century into practice the doctrine that English law should be taught systematically at schools and at the Universities. President Rogers, the chairman of this Section last year, told us that there were then seventy-two schools of law in this country, of which sixty-five were associated with Universities. I am informed upon good authority that the number is now not under seventy-five or seventy-six, and that the proportion of University schools is about the same as that just indicated.

It behoves us now to look squarely at the meaning of these facts, and at the responsibilities that they lay upon us. The most accomplished teachers of law in England have seen with admiration and with something like envy the vantage-ground that has been reached here. We must not be wanting to the position in which we find ourselves. Especially we must not be content with a mere lip service, with merely tagging our law schools with the name of a University, while they lack entirely the University spirit and character. What, then, does our undertaking involve, and that conception of the study of our English system of law, which, in Blackstone's phrase, "extends the pomoeria of University learning and adopts this new tribe of citizens within these philosophical walls"? It means this, that our law must be studied and taught as other great sciences are studied and taught at the Universities, as deeply, by like methods, and with as thorough a concentration and life-long devotion of all the powers of a learned and studious faculty. If our law be not a science worthy and requiring to be thus studied and thus taught, then, as a distinguished lawyer has remarked, "A University will best consult its own dignity in declining to teach it." This is the plough to which our ancestors here in America set their hand and to which we have set ours; and we must see to it that the furrow is handsomely turned.

But who is there, I may be asked, to study law in this way? Who is to have the time for it and the opportunity? Let me ask a question in return, and answer it. Who is it that studies the natural or physical sciences, engineering, philology, history, theology, or medical science in this way? First of all, those who, for any reason, propose to master these subjects, to make true and exact statements of them, and to carry forward in these regions the limits of human knowledge; and especially the teachers of these things. Second, not in so great a degree, but each as far as he may, the leaders in the practical application of these branches of knowledge to human affairs. Third, in a still less degree, yet in some degree, all practitioners of these subjects, if I may use that phrase, who wish to understand their business and to do it thoroughly well.

Precisely the same thing is true in law as in these or any other of the great parts of human knowledge. In all it is alike beneficial, and alike necessary for the vigorous and fruitful development of the subject, for the best performance of the every-day work of the calling to which they relate, and for the best carrying out of the plain practical duties of each man's place, that somewhere and by some persons these subjects should be investigated with the deepest research and the most searching critical study.

The time has gone by when it was necessary to vindicate the utility of deep and lifelong investigations into the nature of electricity and the mode of its operation, into the nature of light and heat and sound and the laws that govern their action, into the minute niceties of the chemical and physiological laboratory, the speculations and experiments of geology, or the absorbing calculations of the mathematician and the astronomer. Men do not now need to be told what it is that has given them the steam-engine, the telegraph, the telephone, the electric railway and the electric light, the telescope, the improved lighthouse, the lucifer match, antiseptic surgery, the prophylactics against small-pox and diphtheria, aluminum the new metal, and the triumphs of modern engineering. These things are mainly the outcome of what seemed to a majority of mankind useless and unpractical study and experiment.

But as regards our law, those who press the importance of thorough and scientific study are not yet exempt from the duty of pointing out the use of it and its necessity. To say nothing of the widespread scepticism among a certain class of practical men, in and out of our profession, as to the advantages of anything of the sort, there is also, among many of those who nominally admit it and even advocate it, a remarkable failure to appreciate what this admission means. It is the simple truth that you cannot have thorough and first-rate training in law, any more than in physical science, unless you have a body of learned teachers; and you cannot have a learned faculty of law unless, like other faculties, they give their lives to their work. The main secret of teaching law, as of all teaching, is what Socrates declared to be the secret of eloquence, understanding your subject; and that requires, as regards any one of the great heads of our law, in the present stage of our science, an enormous and absorbing amount of labor.

Consider how vast the material of our law is, and what the subject-matter is which is to be explored, studied, understood, classified, and taught in our schools of law. It lies chiefly in an immense mass of judicial decisions. These, during several centuries, have spelled out in particular instances, and applied to a vast and perpetually shifting variety of situations, certain inherited principles, formulas, and customs, and certain rules and maxims of good sense and of an ever-developing sense of justice. It lies partly, also, in a quantity of legislation.

What does it mean to ascertain and to master, upon any particular topic, the common law? It means to ascertain and master, in that particular part of it, the true outcome of this body of material. In an old subject, like the law of real property, such an inquiry goes far back. In a new one, like constitutional law, not so far; but still, even in that we must search for more than a century, and if we would have a just understanding of some fundamental matters, it means much remoter and collateral investigation. As regards a great part of our law it is not comprehensible, in the sense in which a legal scholar must comprehend his subject, unless something be known, nay, much, of the great volume of English decisions that run back six hundred years to the days of Edward the First, when English legal reporting begins. That is the period which is fixed, in the two noble volumes of " The History of the English Law " just published by the English professors, Sir Frederick Pollock of Oxford and Mr. Maitland of Cambridge, as the end of their labors; viz., the time when legal reporting begins. In giving the reasons for dealing with this as a separate period, they say " so continuous has been our English legal life during the last six centuries, that the law of the later Middle Ages has never been forgotten among us. It has never passed utterly outside the cognisance of our courts and our practising lawyers." Such is the long tradition that finds expression in the law of this very day, and of this place in which we sit. The volumes just mentioned, ending thus six centuries ago, themselves throw light on much

which concerns our own daily practice in the courts; and they
indicate the value and importance of much remoter investigation.
You remember, perhaps, that the judicial records of England carry
us back to the reign of Richard the First in 1194, seven centuries
ago, and that there are scattered memorials of earlier judicial pro-
ceedings for another century, gathered for the first time by one
of the most learned of our brethren in this association, Prof. Mel-
ville M. Bigelow.

Much of this vast mass of matter is unprinted, and much is in
a foreign tongue. The old records are in Latin. As to the Reports,
for the first two hundred and fifty years after reporting begins, it
is all in the Anglo-French of the Year-Books, and mostly in an
ill-edited and often inaccurate form. To all these sources of diffi-
culty must be added the generally brief and often very uninstruc-
tive shape of the report itself. A few of the earlier Year-Books
have been edited in thorough and scholarly fashion, accompanied
by a translation and illustrations from the manuscript records.
But most of them are in a condition which makes research very
difficult. The learned historians just quoted have said that " the
first and indispensable preliminary to a better legal history than
we have of the later Middle Ages is a new, a complete, a tolerable
edition of the Year-Books. They should be our glory, for no other
country has anything like them; they are our disgrace, for no
other country would have so neglected them." The glory and
disgrace are ours also, for English law is ours. Efforts on both
sides of the water to accomplish this result have as yet failed;
but they should succeed, and they will succeed. I wish that my
voice might reach some one that would help in securing that important result. It would bring down the blessing of legal scholars
now and hereafter. After the Year-Books, come three centuries
and a half of reported cases in England; and one of these centuries, more or less, includes the multitudinous reports of our own
country and of the English colonies, which continue to pour in
upon us daily in so copious and ever-increasing a flood.

Now, will it be said, perhaps, that in bringing forward for study
all this mass of material, past, present, and daily increasing at so
vast a rate, I am recommending an impossibility and an absurdity?
No, I am not ; I speak as one who has seen it tried. It is not only
practicable, but a necessary preliminary for first-rate work. One
or two things must be observed here. Of course no one man can
thus explore all our law. But some single thing or several con-

nected things he may; and every man who proposes really to' understand any topic, to put himself in a position to explain it to others, or to restate it with exactness, must search out that one topic through all its development. Such an investigation calls for much time, patience, and labor, but it brings an abundant harvest in the illumination of every corner of the subject. Another thing is to be noticed. Not all our law runs back through all this period. This great living trunk of the common law sends out shoots all along its length. Some subjects, like the law of real property, crimes, pleading, and the jury go very far back; others, like the learning of Perpetuities or the Statute of Frauds, not so very far; and others still, like our American Constitutional Law, the learning of the Factors' Acts, of injuries to fellow-servants and other parts of the law of torts, are modern, and perhaps very recent. But be the subject old or new, or much or little, every man in his own field of study must explore this mass of material, — viz., all the decided cases relating to it, — if he would thoroughly understand his subject.

Before I pass on, let me say, as if in a parenthesis, a word or two more about the Year-Books. These great repositories of our mediæval law have been the subject of many cheap and foolish observations, as to their mustiness and mouldiness; but never, so far as I know, from persons who had any considerable acquaintance with them. It has dwarfed and hurt our law that research has usually stopped short about three centuries back; as to what went before, it has been the fashion to accept Coke as the epitome, or to take the summaries in the Abridgments. Back of Coke, these ill-printed, unedited, untranslated folios, the Year-Books, have stood like a wall, repelling for most men any further search. But not all scholars have been deterred; and those who have gone through these volumes have found a rich reward. Amidst their quaint and antiquated learning is found the key to many a modern anomaly; and the reader observes with delight the vigorous growth of the law from age to age by just the same processes which work in it to-day in our latest reports. There, as well as here, together with much that is petty and narrow, one remarks not only well-digested learning and thoughtful conservatism giving its reasons, but also growth, the vigor of original thought, liberal ideas, and the breaking out of what we call the modern spirit.

Coming back to the task of the student of our law, it spreads far beyond what I have yet set forth; it has been wisely said that if a man would know any one thing, he must know more than one. And so our system of law must be compared with others; its characteristics only come out when this is done. As to the examination of mediæval and modern continental law, we have hardly made a beginning. When we trace our law far back, the only possible comparison with anything long-lived and continuous is with the Roman law. If any one would remind himself of the flood of light that may come from such comparisons, let him recall the brilliant work of Pollock's predecessor at Oxford, Sir Henry Maine, in his great book on Ancient. Law. That is the best use of the Roman law for us, as a mirror to reflect light upon our own, a tool to unlock its secrets. And so the recent learned historians of our law have used it. In writing of the English system of writs and forms of action, for instance, they put meaning into the whole matter in pointing out that all this, beginning in the middle of the twelfth century, finds a parallel in Rome "at a remote stage of Roman history. We call it distinctively English; but it is also in a certain sense very Roman. While the other nations of Western Europe were beginning to adopt as their own the ultimate results of Roman legal history, England was unconsciously reproducing that history."

Of the value of such comparative studies, and their immense power to lift the different subjects of our law into a clear and animating light, no competent person who has once profited by them can ever doubt. But, again, observe what this means. It means adding to the wide and difficult researches already marked out another great field of investigation. If it be said that our teacher of English law may profit by the labor of others, and has only to read his "Ancient Law," and his "History of English Law," I reply that the field is still largely unexplored; and, furthermore, that, for the scholar, such books are helps and guides for his own research, and not substitutes for it.

So much for this head of what I have to say. Over these vast fields the competent teacher of law must carefully and minutely explore the history and development of his subject. I set down first this thorough historical and chronological exploration, because in this lie hidden the explanation of what is most troublesome in our law, and because in this is found the stimulus that most feeds the enthusiasm and enriches the thought and the instruction of the teacher. The dullest topics kindle when touched with the light of historical research, and the most recondite and technical fall into the order of common experience and rational thought. Sir Henry Maine's book, like that of Darwin in a different sphere, at about the same time, created an epoch. Such books have made it impossible for the law student ever again to be content with the sort of food that fed his fathers, with that "disorderly mass of crabbed pedantry," for instance, as our recent historians of the law have justly called it, "that Coke poured forth as institutes of English law." Never again can he receive the spirit of bondage that once bent itself to teach or to study the law through such a medium.[1]

And now comes another labor for the legal scholar. After such researches as I have indicated, in any part of the law, the outcome of it is certain to be the necessity of restating the subject in hand. When things have once been thus explored and traced, many a hitherto unobserved relationship of ideas comes to light, many an old one vanishes, many a new explanation of current doctrines is suggested and many a disentangling of confused topics, many a clearing away of ambiguities, of false theories, of outworn and unintelligible phraseology. There is no such dissolver and rationalizer of technicality as this. A new order arises. And so when the work of exploration has been gone over, there comes the time for producing and publishing the results of it. Admirable work of this sort, and a good bulk of it, has already been done, — work that is certain to be of inestimable value to our profession. In some instances it is but little known as yet; in others, it appears already in our handbooks on both sides of the ocean, and in the decisions of the courts.

The publishing of these results by competent persons is one of the chief benefits which we may expect from the thorough and scientific teaching of law at the universities. In no respect can more be done to aid our courts in their great and difficult task There are many useful handbooks for office use and reference, and some excellent ones. But the number of really good English law treatises — good, I mean, when measured by a high standard — is very few indeed. They improve; and yet, to a great extent to-day, the writers and publishers of lawbooks are abusing the confidence of the profession, and practising upon its necessities.

---

[1] In saying of Coke what is just quoted, it will be observed that he is dealt with as a writer of institutes of the law. Of course that great name stands for much else in our law and our constitutional history, — for much which is great and good and never to be forgotten.

If I am asked to specify more particularly the sort of thing that may come out of the researches to which I have referred, and that has already been produced from the Universities, I am tempted to refer first to a foreign book about one of our English topics, — a book which is a little remote from our every-day questions, but full of value in any deep consideration of the° subject, — the admirable History of the Jury by Brunner, professor of law at Berlin, published in 1872. That is a book of the first class, superseding all others upon the subject ; and yet, to the disgrace of the English-speaking race, it has not yet been translated into our language. English and American scholars have supplemented the work of Brunner; and the material for a true understanding of the history and uses of the jury system, and for a wise judgment as to continuing or modifying the use of it, were never anything like so good as now.

Then there is that masterly History of the English Law by two English law professors of our own time, of which I have already spoken. In mentioning this book, it is only just to Professor Maitland, one of the finest scholars of our time, that I should quote the remark of his distinguished associate, where he says in the preface that, "although the book was planned in common and has been revised by both of us, by far the greater share of the execution belongs to Mr. Maitland, both as to the actual writing and as to the detailed research which was constantly required." Of other English work to be credited to the Universities, I have already mentioned the great performances of Blackstone and Maine, and I need only allude to the important works, well known among us, of Dicey, Holland, Markby, and Pollock. Less well known, but masterly in its way is Maitland's editing of that selection from the judicial records of the thirteenth century which is known as Bracton's Note Book, and of other unpublished material brought out by the Selden Society.

As to this country, I will not mention names. I need not refer to the famous and familiar books from our University schools of law, by our leaders, living and dead. I will simply say this, that in recent times the researches and contributions of our own teachers of the law, at the Universities in various parts of the country, — and I include now not less than seven of these institutions, — have produced most important material, which is already finding its way into the current handbooks of the profession, here and in England, — material which not only illuminates the field of the student's work, but lightens the daily drudgery of the bench and bar. The true nature of equitable rights and remedies; the doctrine of equitable defences; the history and analysis of the law of Contract, Torts, Trusts, and Evidence; the nature and true theory of the negotiability of obligations; the nature of the Common Law itself; the whole doctrine of Quasi-Contract; the doctrine of Perpetuities, — these things make only a part of this material. As I said, I do not speak of work done at any one institution or in any one part of the country merely.

But now suppose some one says, What is the use of carrying on our backs all this enormous load of the Common Law? Let us codify, and be rid of all this by enacting what we need, and repealing the rest.

Well, I am not going to discuss codification. There is not time for that. And the word is an ambiguous one; some good things and some bad ones are called by this name. I will only say that as yet we do not well understand our law; it is our first duty to understand it. The effort to codify it, or systematically to restate it for purposes of legislation, — for any purpose other than a merely academic one, — should come later, if it come at all. To codify what is only half understood is to perpetuate a mass of errors and shallow ambiguities; it is to begin at the wrong end. Let us, first of all, thoroughly know our ground. I can say this with confidence, that as regards one or two departments of law with which I have a considerable acquaintance, I have never seen any attempt at codification, here or abroad, which was not plainly marked by grave and disqualifying defects. Good-will, strong general capacity, courage, sense, practical gifts, are indeed not wanting in some of these attempts; but a competent knowledge of the subject is wanting.

My honored friend, Judge Dillon, in his excellent address last year, said a word or two in connection with this subject which should be supplemented, I think, by a word or two more. In speaking of law reforms, he remarked that "no mere doctrinaire or closet student of our technical system of law is capable of wise and well-directed efforts to amend it. This must be the work of practical lawyers." If the expression "mere doctrinaire or closet student" refers to any class of pedants and incompetent persons who do not appreciate the nature of what they are studying, I should not wish to qualify that portion of the remark just quoted which reaches them. But if it may be supposed to allude to the class of legal scholars as such, to the experts in legal and juristic learning, this remark, at the best, is but half a truth.   The practical work of carrying through any considerable measure of reform, of getting it enacted, is indeed peculiarly a task for the practical lawyer.   His judgment also is important in the wise shaping of such a measure; as his authority and influence will be quite essential in gaining for it the confidence of legislators and their constituents.   But no "wise and well-directed efforts" of this character can dispense with the approval and co-operation of the legal scholar.   I am speaking, of course, of competent persons, in both the classes referred to, and not of pedants or ignoramuses ; and am assuming on the part of the systematic student of law, as on the part of the judge or practitioner, a suitable outfit of sense, discretion, preliminary professional education, and capacity to understand the eminently practical nature of the considerations which govern the discussion of legal questions.   Perhaps I may be permitted to speak on this subject with the more confidence, as having been a busy practitioner at the bar of a large city for eighteen years, before beginning an experience as a professor at the Harvard Law School which has now continued for twenty-one years.

Professor Dicey has remarked, I believe, of the jurist's work in England, of the sort of work which he himself has so admirably done, that it "stinks in the nostrils" of the average English practitioner ; and Sir Frederick Pollock, in his inaugural lecture, twelve years ago, as Corpus Professor of Jurisprudence at Oxford, in speaking of his associates there, Dicey and Bryce and Anson, says, with dignity, that they are "fellow-workers in a pursuit still followed in this land by few, scorned or depreciated by many, the scientific and systematic study of law."[1]   That state of things is slowly disappearing in England, as well as here, with the gradual improvement in the legal education of the bar.   One of the best and most important results of this improvement will be a more cordial respect and a closer co-operation between the different parts of our profession, the scholars and the men of affairs.   Nothing is more important to the dignity and power of our common calling.

Let me now finally come down to this question : If what I have been saying as to the scope of the work of the University teaching of law be true, what does it mean as regards the outfit and the carrying on of these schools?

---

[1] Oxford Lectures, 38

It means several things. (1) Limiting the task of the instructors. Instead of allotting to a man the whole of the common law, or half a dozen disconnected subjects at once, it means giving him a far more limited field, — one single subject, perhaps; two or three at most; if more than one, then, if possible, nearly related subjects; to the end that his work of instruction may be thoroughly done, and that as the final outcome of his studies some solid, public, and permanent contribution may be made to the main topic which he has in hand.

It means (2) that instructors shall give, substantially, their whole time and strength to the work. In mastering their material and qualifying themselves for their task, they have in hand, say for the next two generations, much formidable labor in exploring the history and chronological development of our law in all its parts. On this, as I have indicated, a brave beginning has been made, and it is already yielding the handsomest fruits. They have also, of course, all the detail of their difficult main work of teaching; and this, when the work is fitly performed, calls for an amount of time, thought and attention bestowed on the personal side of a man's relation to his students which instructors now can seldom give.

It means (3) that the pupils also shall give all their time to the work of legal study while they are about it. There is more than enough in the careful preliminary study of the law to occupy three full years of an able and thoroughly trained young man. It is, I think, a delusion to suppose that this precious seed-time can profitably be employed, in any degree, in attendance upon the courts or in apprenticeship in an office. I do not speak, of course, of an occasional excursion into these regions when some great case is up or some great lawyer is to be heard, or of the occasional continuous use of time in such ways during these long vacations which are generally allowed nowadays. Nor do I mean to deny that attendance upon courts to witness the trial of a case now and then will be a good school exercise. I speak only of systematic attempts to combine attendance at law schools with office-work and with watching the courts. The time for all that comes later, or perhaps in some cases, before.

It means (4) that generous libraries shall be collected at the Universities suited to all the ordinary necessities of careful legal research; and it also means gathering at some one point in the country, or at several points, the best law library that money can possibly buy

And (5), in saying that proper University teaching of law means all this, I am saying in the same breath that it means another thing; viz., the endowment of such schools. The highest education always means endowment; the schools which give it are all charity schools. What student at Oxford or Cambridge, at Harvard, Yale, Columbia, Ann Arbor, or Chicago pays his way? We must recognize, in providing for teaching our great science of the law, that it is no exception to the rule. Our law schools must be endowed as our colleges are endowed. If they are not, then the managers must needs consult the market, and consider what will pay; they will bid for numbers of students instead of excellence of work. They will act in the spirit of a distinguished, but ill-advised trustee of one of the seats of learning in my own State of Massachusetts, when he remarked, "We should run this institution as we would run a mill; if any part of it does not pay, we should lop it off." They will come to forget that it is the peculiar calling of a University to maintain schools that do not pay, or, to speak more exactly, to maintain them whether they pay or not; that the first requisite for the conduct of a University is faith in the highest standards of work; and that if maintaining these standards does not pay, this circumstance is nothing to the purpose, — maintained they must be, none the less. It has been justly said that it is not the office of a University to make money, or even to support itself, but wisely to use money.

If, then, we of the American Bar would have our law hold its fit place among the great objects of human study and contemplation; if we would breed lawyers well grounded in what is fundamental in its learning and its principles, competent to handle it with the courage that springs from assured knowledge, and inspired with love of it, — men who are not, indeed, in any degree insensible to worldly ambitions and emoluments, who are, rather, filled with a wholesome and eager desire for them, but whose minds have been lifted and steadied and their ambitions purged and animated by a knowledge of the great past of their profession, of the secular processes and struggles by which it has been, is now, and ever will be struggling towards justice and emerging into a better conformity to the actual wants of mankind, —then we must deal with it at our Universities and our higher schools as all other sciences and all other great and difficult subjects are dealt with, as thoroughly, and with no less an expenditure of time and money and effort.

James Bradley Thayer.